CONNOISSEUR'S LIBRARY

CHIPPENDALE
and his contemporaries

JOHN KENWORTHY-BROWNE

WORLD PUBLISHING
TIMES MIRROR
NEW YORK

Contents

The colour photographs in this book were taken by
C. A. Cooper (1, 5–9, 12, 15, 20–22, 25, 27, 28, 32–34, 37,
38, 44, 45, 48–61, 69, 70, 74, 78, 79, 83, 85–87, 89–96) and
G. Dagli Orti (2–4, 10, 11, 13, 14, 16–19, 23, 24, 26, 29–31,
35, 36, 39–43, 46, 47, 62–68, 71–73, 75–77, 80–82, 84, 88).
The photographs in the introductory section were supplied by
Carlton Studios and The Cooper-Bridgeman Library

Published by The World Publishing Company
First American edition
First printing—1973
Copyright © Istituto Geografico De Agostini, Novara 1971
English edition © Orbis Publishing Limited, London 1973
All rights reserved
ISBN 0-529-05013-7
Library of Congress catalog card number: 72-10603
Phototypeset in England by Petty and Sons Limited, Leeds
Printed in Italy by IGDA, Novara

Library of Congress cataloging in publication data

Kenworthy-Browne, J A
    Chippendale and his contemporaries.

    (Connoisseur's library)
    Bibliography: p.
    1. Chippendale, Thomas, 1718-1779. 2. Cabinet
workers—England. 3. Decoration and ornament—
Georgian style. I. Title. II. Series: Connoisseur's
library (New York)
NK2529.K45   749.2′2   72-10603
ISBN 0-529-05013-7

WORLD PUBLISHING
TIMES MIRROR

Enterprise and tradition

The golden age of English furniture was the eighteenth century, and particularly the period 1740–1800, when England was established as a formidable power in Europe. One can easily trace the movement back to the 1690s; the country's improved military and naval power, banking and credit systems, and her progressive agricultural methods all witness the economic vigour of this age. By the 1750s England was France's most serious rival, thwarting her policies and stealing her colonies. France had nearly three times the population of England, and contained greater natural resources, but the vitality of England enabled her people to compete with deadly effect.

Yet in sophistication of culture and intellect, France remained undeniably superior. Although they were the declared enemies of France, the fashionable English constantly borrowed French modes in dress, furniture and other arts. On the whole, after 1750, the designers of furniture and other decorative arts watched the styles of Paris more than they studied the ancient classical arts of Rome.

The difference between the British way of life and that of the other powers of Europe was due largely to Britain's method of government. Most of Europe was controlled by autocratic princes (Holland was the most notable exception). But in 1714 the Hanoverian succession to the English throne was deliberately chosen by the Whigs as a court of no effective power and of limited influence; the country was governed by its aristocracy. The system led to a certain ineffectiveness of bureaucratic administration, but this was more than made up for by the spirit of enterprise and personal responsibility that was so vital to the eighteenth and nineteenth centuries. It was entirely through the enterprise of individuals, for instance, that England led the world in the Industrial Revolution from about 1770 onwards. Free enterprise suited the temperament of some foreign artists, as well as the English: George Frederick Handel, probably the most renowned musician in Europe, found the freedom of London more to his taste than protection in the courts of Germany or Italy. Yet he had to struggle against his rivals, and twice he was reduced to bankruptcy. Free enterprise allowed for the meteoric success of a furniture-maker like Thomas Chippendale; it also allowed a near-genius like Sheraton virtually to starve, since he had no guarantee of a living wage. Thus the manufacture of furniture in London was very different from the situation in Paris, where before 1792 the entire trade was strictly regulated by the jealous guild of the *menuisiers-ébénistes*.

English cabinet-makers were under no official restrictions. High traditions of work were maintained because faulty or bad workmanship was not tolerated. But there was no guild to enforce conditions of work; no registry of makers; and no need to qualify as a master of the craft by submitting a finished piece to a jury (as was the practice in Paris). One result of such English *laissez faire* is that furniture was signed only in the rarest cases. Even the practice of pasting the maker's trade card on a finished piece seems to have been uncommon, and very few examples survive. So unless the relevant bill or document happens to have been preserved, most English furniture is anonymous. This can be the case even with pieces of the finest design, materials and workmanship, and even with furniture made for the greatest of great houses. Another result is that, in the absence of any official registration, we know very little of the craftsmen themselves, and their conditions and methods of work. From the London rate lists and other scattered sources, the late Mr Ambrose Heal compiled a book containing names and addresses of about two thousand London makers of furniture and its allied trades, who were working between 1750 and 1800; but barely forty of these are known to us by actual works or reputation.

The complicated business of furniture-making involved a large number of trades. According to the old traditions of the sixteenth century (and earlier), chests and cupboards were made by the joiner, chairs by the turner, or by joiner and turner combined. When, after 1660, under French and Dutch influences, marquetry became the fashion, a specialist cabinet-maker was employed by the joiner to lay the veneers. By about 1700 the cabinet-maker was superior to the joiner, and about the same time chair-making was necessarily a specialized trade. As French and Italian fashions for decorative carved furniture spread, so the carver rose in importance, accompanied by the gilder. Glass makers and glass grinders again were specialists in an age when looking glass was rising in demand but was fragile and enormously expensive. Metalworkers, who cast and chased gilt bronze (ormolu) or brass, supplied decorative handles, locks and hinges. Finally there was the upholsterer. An upholsterer or 'upholder' was more than a man who covered chairs and sofas: in 1747 it was stated that the upholder 'was originally a species of Taylor, but by degrees has . . . set up as a connoisseur in every article that belongs to a House . . . He employs journeymen in his own proper calling, cabinet-makers, glass grinders, looking glass framers, carvers for chairs, the woollen draper, the linen draper, several species of smiths, and a vast army of tradesmen of the other mechanic branches'.

This describes a fully comprehensive furniture manufactory existing before 1750. Presumably it applied to some makers of that period that we actually know, like Benjamin Goodison, or William Linnell. It was after 1750 that Thomas Chippendale gained importance on the scene, when he quickly rose to be the 'complete decorator' of the description shown above.

The name of Thomas Chippendale the elder (1718–79) has become almost synonymous with the mid-Georgian style because of the great pattern book, *The Gentleman and Cabinet-Maker's Director*, published by him in 1754. It had 161 folio plates, this number being increased to 200 in the third edition of 1762. Nothing on this scale had appeared in England (or elsewhere) before, and although it provoked a number of rival publications, nothing approaching the same range of patterns appeared again until Hepplewhite's book of 1788. The *Director* is still impressive for many reasons: for its comprehensiveness, illustrating nearly all kinds of furniture; for the range and fluency of its designs, passing in style from classical, through French (rococo), chinoiserie and gothic; and, not least, for the excellence of its engraving and production.

Chippendale's enterprise in compiling the book was extraordinary. His purpose was to gain clients and a large volume of business, and there is no doubt that it was a masterpiece of advertising. He had courage as well as technical knowledge and organising ability. We know almost nothing of his career up to 1753, when he bought the lease of two adjacent houses in St Martin's Lane, presumably anticipating a great business; and a third house was added later. Somehow he collected a long and impressive list of subscribers for his first edition among both aristocracy and craftsmen, and he wrote: 'The Titlepage has already called the work *The Gentleman and Cabinet-Maker's Director*, as being calculated to assist the one in the choice, and the other in the execution of the designs'. Chippendale's business grew as he had foreseen. Himself trained as a cabinet-maker, he took as partner for a while James Rannie (who was an 'upholder'), and his houses were organized to contain nearly all the branches of the manufacture, with dwelling rooms above.

Although it is obvious that Chippendale quickly gained many influential clients, we do not know many actual examples of his work before the 1760s. However at Nostell Priory (c.1766–70) and Harewood House (c.1770–5), both situated in Yorkshire, there survive bills and letters to document specific pieces of furniture, and to furnish proof that he had been supplying these houses for some years before and after the above dates. The furniture itself is distinctive enough, but more than this, it is proved that at these two houses, as elsewhere, Chippendale acted as the complete decorator or upholder, assisting with paper-hanging and curtaining.

If Chippendale was one of the most enterprising and ambitious furniture makers, this does not mean that he was necessarily the best. It could be that his business ability was greater than his craftsmanship; but the situation became complicated as he employed many artists and craftsmen of high calibre in his business. Sadly, he did not make a fortune, but was constantly pressed for money, as his patrons did not always deem it necessary to pay him promptly. Perhaps because of his unmistakable and droll name, more information has been published about Chippendale than about his contemporaries. Among other fine makers, William and John Linnell worked in a corner of Berkeley Square in Mayfair (the newest and most fashionable district of London), where they made fine chairs and carved mirrors. Thomas Johnson, in Soho and Seven Dials, was an outstanding carver in the rococo style, as well as an advanced designer. Ince and Mayhew, in partnership in Soho, had an important and noble clientele, and published a small book in 1762 imitating the *Director* – as did Robert Manwaring, a chair-maker, in the 1760s. But the finest maker of the period has generally been considered to be William Vile, whose partner was John Cobb.

From 1750, Vile's premises were in St Martin's Lane, only ten doors north from Chippendale. Few documents have come to light bearing his name, but he is known to have made furniture for The Vyne, and for King George III. Several documented pieces in the royal collection show the excellent quality of his work. In style he tended chiefly to be traditional and to avoid the excesses of the rococo and chinoiserie fashions, both of which Chippendale had illustrated fully and with considerable invention.

Palladian is the word used for the rather severe architecture practised by Lord Burlington, William Kent and others from about 1720 onwards. In fact their style seldom has much close resemblance to Palladio's palaces or villas in the Veneto region of North Italy. Rather, it was an attempt to build according to the principles of the first-century Roman architect Vitruvius, and according to the excellence of ancient Rome. Palladio's *Quattro Libri dell'Architettura* (1570) expounded more clearly and simply than any other treatise the classical principles, which in Vitruvius's books remained obscure. Since Palladio's own buildings retain a classical purity not found in later Italian architecture, the English neo-Palladians read Vitruvius's

Artists and craftsmen working in the St Martin's Lane area c.1740–70. (Shown on Horwood's Map of London, 1799.) 1. Thomas Chippendale (cabinet-maker); 2. L-F. Roubiliac (sculptor); 3. William Hallett (cabinet-maker); 4. William Vile and John Cobb (cabinet-makers); 5. Matthias Lock (designer and engraver); 6. Thomas Johnson (carver); 7. Old Slaughter's Coffee House; 8. James Paine (architect); 9. John Gwynne (architect); 10. Robert Edge Pyne (painter); 11. Powel's Colour Shop; 12. Francis Hayman (painter); 13. The St Martin's Lane Academy; 14. Peter Channon (cabinet-maker); 15. John Bradburn (cabinet-maker); 16. Matthew Darley (engraver); 17. William Hogarth (painter); 18. Leicester House, residence of Frederick, Prince of Wales; 19. Sir Joshua Reynolds (painter)

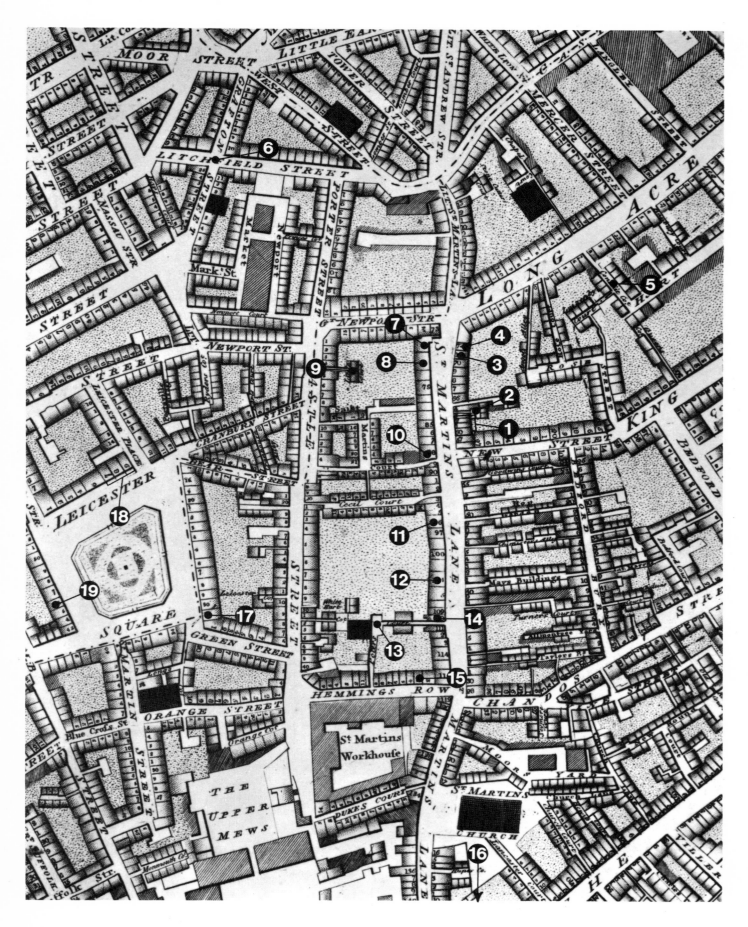

ten books like the Old Testament, and Palladio's *Quattro Libri* like the New. Several editions of Palladio appeared in English during the eighteenth century.

Palladianism in England had political overtones. The Whig aristocracy had established the Protestant and almost powerless Hanoverian succession in 1714, in preference to the legitimate but despotic Stuarts. Having satisfactorily settled their form of government, they felt that England was now the proper heir to the republican traditions of Ancient Rome. They avoided the enthusiasms of baroque, which they associated with Catholic absolutism, and built and furnished in a purer (as they thought) classical manner. Examples of the true classical style were found in the ruined temples of Rome and translated by people like William Kent, who built at Houghton and Holkham. Kent was an architect-decorator, and the magnificence of Rome appeared not only in the façades of the buildings but also in superb suites of state rooms, in the rich wall-colouring and sumptuous furniture that he designed as well.

Chippendale himself had no doubt of the value of architectural training to the furniture-maker. The first plates in the *Director* analyze the five orders of architecture, which he declared to be 'the very soul and basis of his (the cabinet-maker's) art'. Furniture designers in the eighteenth century, seldom forgot the classical rules, and because of this English furniture consistently kept its good and pleasing proportions. The Palladian tradition remained the normal style in architecture and furniture up to and beyond 1760; but by the *Director* year of 1754, the splendour and ponderous magnificence were already greatly tempered down. Forms had become less heavy, and contours less severe. A bookcase, for instance, might be constructed like a building, even with a plinth course, columns and entablature, all in their proper classical proportions, but it was relieved with light carvings of acanthus leaves, festoons of flowers, or shaped panel borders incorporating various mouldings, leaf-clasps and *paterae*. Such decoration applied or carved in solid mahogany, became ever lighter, smaller and more refined. At the same time, a curvaceous rococo tendency was making the contours of Palladianism gentle and serpentine.

Rococo with variations

Chippendale wished to show himself an expert in all the newest fashions. Not only did he employ two designers and engravers for his book who were already fluent in principles of rococo design – namely Matthias Lock and Matthew Darly – but he also took premises in St Martin's Lane, which was then the centre of the rococo movement.

Nowadays we would call the atmosphere of St Martin's Lane 'bohemian' or 'off-beat'. In it there was little rapport with the Palladian-minded Whig aristocracy and their serious ideals; here there lived numerous artists, actors, painters, engravers and craftsmen, printsellers and furniture-makers. Their favoured café was Old Slaughter's Coffee House, almost opposite Chippendale's premises, and it was here that the rococo took root in England. Among this company there was the French designer and engraver Gravelot, who lived in England from 1732 to 1746. His work was in the full rococo idiom of Meissonnier, and first the artists, and then the craftsmen learnt from him.

Matthias Lock adapted French rococo to furniture designs from 1740, handling the rococo with an assurance and even brilliance that was never equalled in England, and Chippendale did well to employ him. But Chippendale also claimed to have designed and drawn many of his examples himself.

By the *Director* period the designs were settling down to something of a national English rococo idiom. The typical 'Chippendale' or rococo mirror translates into three-dimensional carving what in France might have been intended for ormolu, or merely for engraving. *Director* rococo is certainly elaborate, but still more elaboration was possible. The designs of Thomas Johnson, published between 1755 and 1761, seem too fantastic to be carried out in wood, but Johnson, who was by trade a carver, asserted that his patterns 'may all be performed by a Master of his Art', and that he could execute them himself. One may note in passing that the designs of Johnson, and indeed of Lock, seem to contain features that are also to be found in German rococo. This has not yet been explained.

In contrast to Johnson's florid designs, John Linnell worked in a more laconic style. It is known that he had learnt design in St Martin's Lane, but his drawings and the pieces known to have been made by him are simpler and more geometrical than Johnson's, showing smooth contours rather than nervous chiselling. Normally these carvers' pieces were to be made in soft wood and gilded, but on chairs and commodes cabinet-makers performed marvels out of the excessively hard mahogany. Rococo scrollwork was originally copied from French designs for ormolu and metalwork, and when executed in solid dark wood it no longer looked particularly French. As in Johnson's designs, many of the rococo pieces in the *Director* appear fantastic, but a number of examples survive to show that they were indeed carried out.

The simultaneous fashion for chinoiserie is well illustrated throughout the *Director*. Chinoiserie was a decorative style, for the essential structure of such pieces remained English and not at all oriental. It was fantasy or make-believe, an attempt to recreate the supposed delights of distant Cathay in domestic life. Its natural accompaniment was tea-drinking out of porcelain cups, and chinoiserie was therefore most suitable for ladies' boudoirs or bedrooms. The decorative motifs originated in luxury goods imported from China, either lacquered screens and cabinets, or the beautifully coloured wallpapers that normally formed the basis of a Chinese room.

The English imitation of lacquer was known as 'Japan' work, and very often it was a good imitation of the genuine Chinese article. On the other hand, it was necessary to invent new forms for Chinese chairs, cabinets, mirrors and other forms of carved furniture. To the Chinese such pieces would not seem at all oriental, and indeed they were ridiculed at the time. It seemed enough to carve European peasants with long moustaches and pointed hats, or to add to a group a Chinese paling or pagoda: in construction (and often in design) such pieces remained resolutely rococo. Chairs and display shelves were called 'Chinese' when filled in with Chinese frets, and covered with canopied crestings. Such pieces bore no resemblance to oriental furniture, yet

An elaborate design for a dressing table. The work of Thomas Chippendale the elder, and published in 1761

Design for a Toylet Table

T. Chippendale inv.t et delin.   Publish'd according to Act of Parliam.t 1761.   W. Foster Sculp.

they remained more fashionable than the few attempts to introduce genuine Chinese styles by those who had actually seen them in Canton.

This kind of furniture, popularly known today as 'Chinese Chippendale' is charming if absurd, and has no parallel outside England. Neither has the rather similar 'gothic' style. Whereas chinoiserie was a feminine diversion, whimsical and exotic, gothic was more masculine and literary, turning a nostalgic eye to the medieval past. Around 1750 it was favoured by men of letters like Horace Walpole and the poet Thomas Gray, and by 1790 the gothic revival had the impulse of the Romantic movement. For the moment, however, it was thought suitable for poetry, decorative ruins, libraries, dining rooms and bachelor apartments.

Until the nineteenth century the true nature of the gothic was very imperfectly understood. In practice, Georgian gothic furniture, like the Chinese, is distinguished only by the use of medieval details rather than Palladian or rococo. A gothic bookcase or chair is of the familiar Georgian structure but carved with pointed arches, quatre-foil panels and crocket pinnacles. 'Bastard gothic' is not a true style, any more than 'mongrel Chinese'; both were English variations of rococo.

Rococo in England had unsound roots. It found a few francophile patrons, but not enough properly to establish it, and it remained a movement of the arts and crafts. When Adam launched his neoclassical revolution, he attracted wealthy aristocratic patronage, and rococo withered more quickly in England than in any other European country. Chippendale must have foreseen this, for in 1766 he held a large sale of 'a great variety of fine Cabinet Work', together with a stock of mahogany and other woods. Chinoiserie and gothic were eclipsed too, the first totally, the other partially, but both re-appeared in splendour around the turn of the century. Meanwhile the craftsmen, Chippendale, Linnell, Lock and others continued under the revived classical style as successfully as they had worked during the rococo period.

The neoclassic and Robert Adam

While the rococo was still exercising its charms, the novelty of neoclassical architecture and decoration began to appeal to the more scholarly and educated sections of society. Like rococo, neoclassicism was an international movement, taken up first by the French and English, but inspired by Italy, and especially (in matters of decoration) by the new excavations at Herculaneum and Pompeii, where from 1738 true ancient rooms were being discovered. First-century paintings and plasterwork were exposed, together with domestic objects in bronze and some furniture. For the first time there was evidence of household decoration, which clearly had not followed the Vitruvian rules or the temple style. A truly domestic but nonetheless classical style was now known to have existed.

If the French were in fact the first in making neoclassical furniture (in 1757-8), however, the English were not far behind. The architect James Stuart made drawings dated 1759 for Spencer House in London, which show a rather mixed version of Pompeian-type wall decoration, together with fully neoclassical side tables and other furnishings. 'Athenian' Stuart (1715-88) studied in Rome from 1742, visited Naples in 1748, and made his important study of Greek ruins in 1753-5. His subsequent career as architect and author was rather spasmodic and indolent, and he seldom designed furniture. But he was the pioneer in England of the neoclassical style, and especially of the revival of the true Greek orders in architecture.

Robert Adam (1728-92) and his two rather less talented brothers claimed the entire credit for launching the new style into England: a claim, therefore, that was not entirely justified. Robert studied in Italy from 1754-7. On his return it took him a few years (certainly until 1760) before he reached confidence in the architectural style which he made his own. Generally, he designed his classical decorations to be in very low relief, arranged with geometrical precision and great delicacy. Adam's style was lighter and more delicate than the contemporary neoclassical work in France and Italy: very often he set his ceilings and walls with small, jewel-like paintings of classical scenes, especially painted by Kauffmann or Cipriani, and, somewhat tentatively at first but soon more boldly, his ceilings and walls were painted in exquisitely matched colours and contrasted tones, heightened with a judicious and restrained use of gilding. Heretofore, as he said, plasterwork had been uniformly white, but now, 'the massive entablature, the ponderous compartment ceiling, the tabernacle frame . . . are universally exploded; in their place we have adopted a beautiful variety of light mouldings, gracefully formed, delicately enriched and arranged with propriety and skill'. It was later said by John Soane that Adam caused 'a revolution of electric power', and it is true that all fashionable architects and furniture-makers were very soon forced to work in accordance with it.

The general aspects of the Adam decorations are important to furniture because, even more than those of William Kent, Adam's great rooms were designed as a unity. Whereas Kent had tended to be sombre, ponderous and monumental, Adam now appeared sparkling, elegant and delicate. The furniture fitted the architectural spirit of the room. Decorative pieces in gilded wood, wall mirrors and side tables, required his architect's authority, but he also made patterns for carpets, chairs, commodes and occasionally cabinets, designing their minutest details and 'giving an elegance and an importance to the Keyhole of a Lady's Escritoire'.

Adam did not reach his furniture style easily. He used the form of neoclassical table that had already been invented by Stuart (and the French) and in 1764 he designed a window stool with much the same contour. But otherwise his earliest furniture drawings lie somewhere between baroque and classical, and it was not until about 1767 that he became fluent in inventing new classical forms for furniture.

During the earlier 1760s Adam clearly relied upon the furniture-makers not only to carry out his drawing, but also to advise him on furniture design. During an early collaboration with John Linnell, the architect learnt the principles of chair-making, while the cabinet-maker absorbed those of neoclassicism. John Linnell thereafter continued his practice as a carver and chair-maker, and a large collection of his drawings have fortunately been preserved. He developed as personal a style in the neo-classical period as he had formerly in rococo, and his mirror designs, with their use of portrait medallions and chains of husks, have a very distinctive character.

In Adam houses generally there is found a quantity of 'Adam' furniture that cannot be attributed to the architect himself. Clearly the furniture-makers were quick to learn the Adam principles of taste. The firm of Ince and Mayhew, formerly known for rococo chairs, supplied classical pieces to Lord Coventry, one of Adam's important early patrons, from 1765; and by 1770 even such former rococo pioneers as Lock and Darly were making designs in the classical manner with great success. Thomas Chippendale is an interesting case. At Nostell Priory he was clearly copying Adam in a lyre-back chair of 1768, while the furniture he supplied to Harewood House is virtually without equal in England. There are at Harewood several sets of armchairs in a French style (and possibly of French joinery), rather overloaded with classical decoration, but his marquetry furniture made for the same house around 1770 is nothing less than superb in its design, materials and workmanship. These pieces, and a few others similar elsewhere, have been said to rival in quality that of the best *ébénistes* of Paris. They are of plain classical shapes, inlaid with the Adam repertory of ornament; but no Adam designs for these are known, and they are considered to be the unaided work of Chippendale and his firm.

'Adam' furniture, therefore, may look a simple and homogeneous style, but it presents many unsolved problems of design and attribution. Unless there actually exists an autographed drawing, it is dangerous to attribute the design of any furniture in an Adam house to its architect. A particularly interesting case is that of the Tapestry Rooms, of which there exist four in Adam houses (and three others). For these, sets of Gobelins tapestry of a special new pattern were ordered from Paris to cover the walls, chairs and sofas. The architectural details of the rooms were all by Adam himself, and until recently it was never questioned that he had designed the accompanying medallion-back chairs. Now, however, it has been shown that in all probability the general pattern of these chairs was supplied by the Gobelins factory, and that the first of the sets of chairs was made by Ince and Mayhew for Croome Court in 1764. (These last are now in the Metropolitan Museum of Art, New York.)

Robert Adam continued to create sumptuous interiors, and during the 1770s his designs for furniture became numerous. His style showed subtle changes. About 1772, it was over-refined and filigree; after 1778, it lost its clear definition and boldness of character, and he subsequently designed very little furniture. For by now, not only had he attracted formidable rivals in his own style (including the much younger James Wyatt and Henry Holland), but the style itself was severely criticized by its former champions. Horace Walpole scornfully referred to its 'gingerbread and snippets of embroidery', and 'filigraine and fan painting', and although he liked the magnificence of the tapestry room at Osterley, in 1778 he found Adam's latest novelty, the 'Etruscan' room, unworthy of that house. It seems that Walpole was finding, beneath Adam's classical surface decoration, a heart of rococo.

There remain some six houses with complete furnished interiors much as Adam left them; to us they are among the most delightful of English country houses. Over a dozen others have been more or less dismantled. The very rich aristocracy had, for twenty years, found in him the complete architect-decorator they needed, and as such he had no real successor.

Elegance and fashion

As the aristocracy still increased in wealth and grandeur, the middle classes began to make quick fortunes in the industrial provinces, and even the smaller bankers and merchants developed an ambition to live like nobility. Their manners and houses acquired, to a greater or lesser extent, the customs, elegancies and affectations of higher society. Much petty snobbery came from these aspirations, and the resulting social climbing is brilliantly described in the novels of Jane Austen. The increased demand for suitably elegant furniture resulted, on the one hand, in competent cabinet-makers setting up successful centres outside London. The firm of Gillow in Lancaster is the best known of these. Established as early as the 1730s, Gillow's business increased enormously later in the century, and he enjoyed a large export trade. At the same time the traditional country furniture made by the joiner and turner in oak and other native woods was replaced by cabinet-makers' work of both good and indifferent quality, copying the recent fashion in London.

In 1788 two books of furniture designs appeared; one was written exclusively for cabinet-makers, and contained 29 plates by Thomas Shearer. The other became the better known. Called *The Cabinet-Maker and Upholsterer's Guide*, it was a comprehensive collection of designs aspiring to the dimensions of Chippendale's *Director* (which by now was outmoded), and was published by the firm of Hepplewhite.

George Hepplewhite worked in Cripplegate, an unfashionable part of London. Apart from his book, no bill or document or piece of furniture is known by him; and yet the style of the 1780s is universally known by his name. Hepplewhite furniture is, in essentials, a cheaper, less exacting, less scholarly, and, more middle-class version of the Adam style. It also shows the later development of the style that Adam had established. Thus we find the Adam medallion-back chair developed into the shield-back chair, a fine form representative of English furniture design. Adam's uncompromising lines, circles and ovals were now eased into gentle serpentine lines, curved feet and simple undemanding shapes. Hepplewhite's book illustrates useful furniture for the well-to-do, but not for the connoisseur. On the other hand, when one studies the illustrations to *The Guide*, it is clear that high standards in general were maintained by the cabinet-makers in their use of marquetry and other techniques, and that the chair-makers had maintained considerable refinement and technical skill in design and joinery.

The eighteenth century nears its close with the designs of Thomas Sheraton (1751–1806). Sheraton had served an apprenticeship as a cabinet-maker, but when he came to London about 1790 he practised as a drawing master. *The Cabinet-Maker and Upholsterer's Drawing Book* (1791–4) first appeared in parts, but neither this important

work nor two more books produced after 1800 brought him much money. Yet in spite of deep poverty, Sheraton seems to have kept ahead of and even to have dictated the fashion of his day. He lived in Soho, which by now was the home of a great part of the furniture trade, and although he borrowed designs from other makers, many of his drawings appear to be of his own invention. A useful contact was, apparently, the francophile architect Henry Holland, who had rebuilt and furnished Carlton House for the Prince of Wales. Carlton House contained several pieces of Louis XVI furniture as well as Holland's own simplified versions of the French style, and this may be the prime source of the French characteristics that are apparent in so many of Sheraton's plates. He illustrated, for instance, such details as recessed and ornamented colonnettes, minute classical borders and *toupé* feet, clearly derived from the Parisian furniture of Weisweiler, Benemann and Carlin. But when one sees the similar pieces that were actually made, they no longer appear French, for they have nothing of the Parisian richness of kingwood or mahogany, set off by ormolu and Sèvres porcelain. A Sheraton commode or writing cabinet is a fragile, feminine thing, covered with plainly figured but exquisitely contrasted woods. The delicate ornamentation might be carved or inlaid; and quite often it is painted.

Not all of Sheraton's patterns were elaborate. Some indeed were quite simple, and some hardly distinguishable from those of Shearer or Hepplewhite. But Sheraton's superior draughtsmanship invariably gave them a more chic and fashionable appearance. He possessed a more practical mind than one might suppose from his exacting designs, and delighted in mechanical furniture: a table opens up into library steps, complete with folding hand-rail and book-rest, or a 'harlequin' writing table with pop-up pigeon holes is shown with all its complicated mechanics, which Sheraton himself compared to stage scenery.

Sheraton in 1792 was scornful of Hepplewhite's *Guide*, writing of it 'this work has already caught the decline, and, perhaps, in a little time will suddenly die in disorder'. Yet in spite of Hepplewhite's inferior draughtsmanship, and his lack of fashion sense, it is the *Guide* rather than the *Drawing Book* that has survived as typical of the English style in furniture. Hepplewhite's chairs and secretaires, his sideboards and bookcases, remained for over a hundred years a model of useful and agreeable furniture; while Sheraton's inventions, so much more fashionable in their own day, look affected and impractical when reproduced in any other.

We know very little about the furniture workshops during this period, but there does exist a description of a large manufactory, that of George Seddon, who worked at Aldgate in the City of London. This was written by a German traveller, Sophie von la Roche, in her diary for 1786. Seddon, we learn, employed four hundred apprentices who included mirror workers, carpet fitters and

Facing page: Designs by Robert Adam, published in 1772.
Below: Design for a commode, by Thomas Sheraton, 1794

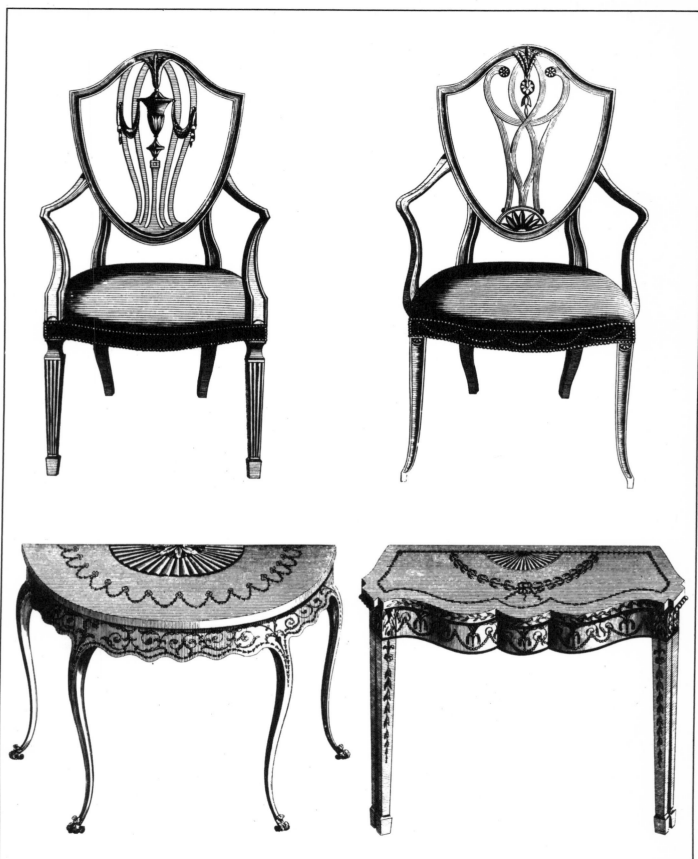

Four typical designs – two chairs and two pier tables – taken from Hepplewhite's 'Guide', published in London from 1788–94

locksmiths, besides all the necessary cabinet-makers for every kind of household furniture. He had his own saw-houses well stocked with native and exotic woods: 'the entire story of the wood, as used for both inexpensive and costly furniture can be traced in this establishment'. With a woman's eye, the diarist gloated over all varieties of chairs and sofas, writing, dressing and toilet tables, cupboards and close stools, and fabrics, in fact 'everything one might desire for furnishing a house'. No other factory is known to have been so great as Seddon; but the house of Gillow in Lancaster, who also had London premises from 1760, was steadily rising in importance. In 1794, Gillow's furnished Streatham House for Mrs Piozzi 'in modern style, supremely elegant, but not expensive'. At this time, Gillow's was the only firm regularly to stamp its name on its furniture. As their practice grew they developed a lively export trade, notably with the West Indies.

In contrast with these successful enterprises, it is sad to end the period with the demise of the house of Chippendale. Thomas Chippendale junior (1749–1822) had taken on the firm on his father's death. He was an artist and clearly more of a dreamer than his energetic father. Financial difficulties seem to have estranged him from Haig, his father's partner, and in 1804 he was declared bankrupt. A five-day sale in St Martin's Lane disposed of his stock of furniture and rare woods, with 'beautiful mahogany cabinet work of the first class including many articles of great taste and of the finest workmanship'. In spite of his troubles, Chippendale junior possessed and maintained 'a very great degree of taste, with great ability as a draughts-man and designer'. His work after 1800 at Stourhead and elsewhere shows that he could be bold, original and even magnificent. Some years after his bankruptcy, as late as 1812, he completed a suite of furniture that shows that had he been able to carry on, his invention would certainly have been equal to the vigorous spirit of the Regency.

Principal woods used

English furniture of about 1740–70 differs from that of all other countries in its universal use of mahogany, a very expensive wood imported from the western colonies. San Domingo mahogany (c.1730–50) was heavy and dark, allowing for vigorous carving often reminiscent of chased bronze. Cuba mahogany (c.1750–80) was less hard, of a red colour and often possessing the 'flame' figure that was generally used for veneered surfaces. Honduras mahogany (from c.1800) was much lighter in weight and colour.

From the Adam period (c.1765–1800) satinwood was more popular than mahogany (though mahogany was still usual for dining rooms). Satinwood was even more expensive. It came from Porto Rico, and was of a pale straw colour with hardly any figure. A less usual variety from the East Indies (much used however during the nineteenth century) was warmer in tone and with a flame figure. The other decorative woods for veneers or contrasting bandings were: tulipwood, Brazilian rosewood, purplewood or amaranth (less common, but used for contrasting back-grounds in panels), and kingwood. Some native woods were also used: harewood is sycamore stained a dull olive green and has a 'fiddle-back' figure; figured yew was popular during the Hepplewhite period. Birch offered a cheaper alternative to satinwood. Marquetry designs were usually in holly, pearwood (often stained green), cherry, plum and ebony.

Dining chairs were normally made from mahogany, but painted furniture was generally of beech. Carved and gilded furniture was of pine. The cheapest case furniture was veneered or painted on a deal carcase, while pine, beech and other softwoods were used for better quality pieces. Cedar was occasionally used for drawer linings. The finest furniture often had mahogany carcase and linings.

Select bibliography

Boynton, L., and Goodison, N., Two articles on 'The Furniture of Thomas Chippendale at Nostell', *Burlington Magazine*, London May and June 1969.

Brackett, O., *Thomas Chippendale*, Hodder & Stoughton, London 1924.

Chippendale, T., *The Gentleman and Cabinet-Maker's Director*, first edition 1754; third edition 1762; reduced facsimile of third edition, Dover Publications Inc., New York 1966

Coleridge, A., *Chippendale Furniture*, Faber & Faber, London 1968.

Edwards, R., *The Shorter Dictionary of English Furniture*, Country Life, Feltham 1964.

Edwards, R., and Jourdain, M., *Georgian Cabinet-Makers*, Country Life, Feltham 1944.

Fastnedge, R., *English Furniture Styles, 1500–1830*, Penguin Books, Harmondsworth 1955.

Fastnedge, R., *Sheraton Furniture*, Faber & Faber, London 1962.

Girouard, M., Three articles on the English Rococo, *Country Life*, Feltham (3rd January, 27th January, 3rd February) 1966.

Harris, E., *The Furniture of Robert Adam*, Tiranti, London 1963.

Harris, E., 'Robert Adam and the Gobelins', *Apollo Magazine*, London April 1962.

Hayward, H., *Thomas Johnson and English Rococo*, Tiranti, London 1964.

Hayward, H., 'The Drawings of John Linnell in the Victoria and Albert Museum', *Furniture History* (vol. v), Furniture History Society, Victoria and Albert Museum, London 1969

Musgrave, C., *Adam and Hepplewhite and other Neoclassical Furniture*, Faber & Faber, London 1966.

Sheraton, T., *The Cabinet-Maker and Upholsterer's Drawing Book*, 1791–4; facsimile reprint, Praeger, New York 1970.

Tomlin, M., *English Furniture*, Faber & Faber, London 1972.

Ward-Jackson, P., *English Furniture Designs of the Eighteenth Century*, Her Majesty's Stationery Office, London 1958.

Wills, G., *English Furniture 1550–1760*, Guinness Superlatives, Enfield 1971.

Chippendale and his contemporaries

DATE	NAME	TRADE	PUBLICATIONS
1686–1748	WILLIAM KENT	architect, painter, landscape gardener, decorator and designer	
fl. 1740–70	MATTHIAS LOCK	designer, engraver, carver (employed by Chippendale)	*A New Drawing Book of Ornaments, Shields, Compartments, Masks, etc.*, (c.1740) and others
1718–79	THOMAS CHIPPENDALE	cabinet-maker	*The Gentleman and Cabinet-Maker's Director*, 1754–62
fl. 1759–1800	WILLIAM INCE and THOMAS MAYHEW	cabinet-makers and upholsterers	*Universal System of Household Furniture*, 1759–63
c.1765	ROBERT MANWARING	chair-maker and cabinet-maker	*The Cabinet-Maker's and Chair-Maker's Real Friend and Companion*, 1765, and others
fl. 1755–62	THOMAS JOHNSON	carver and designer	*Twelve Girandoles*, 1755 *One Hundred and Fifty New Designs*, 1761
d. 1768 d. 1778	WILLIAM VILE JOHN COBB	cabinet-makers and upholsterers (partnership)	
d. 1763 d. c.1798	WILLIAM LINNELL JOHN LINNELL	designers, carvers, cabinet-makers and upholsterers	
1713–1788	JAMES STUART	architect and designer	*The Antiquities of Athens*, 1762, 1787, 1795
1728–92	ROBERT ADAM	architect and designer	*The Works in Architecture* (3 vols), 1773, 1777, 1822
1730–94	JAMES ADAM	brother and partner of Robert Adam	
In England c.1758	MICHELE ANGELO PERGOLESI	decorator, first employed by Adam brothers	*Original Designs*, 1777–1801
fl. c.1760–70	PETER LANGLOIS	cabinet-maker	
1703–73 d. 1811	ROBERT GILLOW RICHARD GILLOW	cabinet-maker son of Robert Gillow and partner from 1757	
d. 1786	GEORGE HEPPLEWHITE	cabinet-maker	*The Cabinet-Maker and Upholsterer's Guide*, 1788–94, (posthumous)
c.1788	THOMAS SHEARER	cabinet-maker and designer	Plates for *The Cabinet-Maker's London Book of Prices*, 1788–93
1727–1801	GEORGE SEDDON	cabinet-maker	
1751–1806	THOMAS SHERATON	drawing master, author and designer	*Cabinet-Maker and Upholsterer's Drawing Book*, 1791–4; *Cabinet Dictionary*, 1803
1749–1822	THOMAS CHIPPENDALE THE YOUNGER	cabinet-maker	

About half the pieces of furniture shown on the following pages still remain in the houses for which they were made. A special debt of gratitude is due to their possessors, who have so generously allowed their rooms and furniture to be photographed – many of them to be reproduced here in colour for the first time. Holkham Hall, Norfolk, the property of the Earl of Leicester, is by William Kent; Corsham Court, Wiltshire, belonging to Lord Methuen, has a rare collection that covers the transition from rococo to Adam. Two houses in Yorkshire, Nostell Priory, the home of Lord St Oswald, and Harewood House, that of the Earl and Countess of Harewood, occupy a special place in this book, for they have documented furniture supplied by Chippendale himself. Osterley Park, Middlesex, has been chosen to illustrate the work of Robert Adam, and Stourhead, Wiltshire, for its work by the younger Chippendale. At other houses, such as The Vyne and Dyrham Park, there are pieces in successive styles that were obtained as different generations of the family furnished a few rooms at a time.

Almost every piece illustrated is to be seen in a house or museum that is open to the public. The last three houses mentioned above belong to the National Trust, while Osterley is cared for by the Victoria and Albert Museum. To them, and to the British Museum Print Room, the Leeds City Art Gallery at Temple Newsam, the London Museum, the Lord Chamberlain's office, Mallett and Son of Bond Street, and Sir John Soane's Museum, thanks are returned for their help and kindness in allowing their property to be illustrated.

1 William Hogarth (1697–1764). *Mariage à la Mode*, scene II. National Gallery, London.

The series of six paintings entitled *Mariage à la Mode*, painted by Hogarth in 1743, tell the tragic story of an 'arranged' marriage. The second picture (shown here) is called 'The Breakfast Scene'. Hogarth's works offer important illustrations of their period, and as he lived in Leicester Square near St Martin's Lane he had a good knowledge of furniture that was made there. This picture shows an interior very much in the Palladian style, with a formal fireplace and correctly proportioned classical columns forming a screen to the room beyond. Strangely, however, most of the furniture is not in the fashion of 1743, but rather that of about twenty years before. In the background there are side chairs with padded seats and backs, and folding card tables on cabriole legs, while the scrolled legs of the tripod table might even be seventeenth century. On the floor there is a valuable Persian carpet.

2 The saloon, Holkham Hall, Norfolk.

Holkham Hall, in Norfolk, remains today very much as it was built, and is a fine example of the Palladian style house. Designed by its owner, the Earl of Leicester, with assistance from the Earl of Burlington and William Kent, it was built over the period 1730–60. It is likely that Kent himself was responsible for furnishing the interior.

The architects were careful to observe mathematical proportions, difficult though this was in a house where all rooms on the same floor must keep to the same height. The saloon (c.1740) measures 40 by 28 feet, and is 32 feet high, thus forming (almost) a cube and a half. Its ceiling details are from Desgotetz's engravings of the Basilica of Constantine in Rome (known to Palladio as the Temple of Peace). The doorway has classical mouldings, and its simple curved pediment gives variety to the prevailing straight lines. On either side of the doorway there is a fireplace of Sicilian marble, and the walls are hung with an expensive Genoese cut velvet.

The furniture in this rich but sober room was almost certainly designed by Kent around 1735. The chairs are simple, even severe. Their scrolled legs are carved with acanthus leaves and scale-pattern, and the seats and backs are covered in flowered Genoese velvet. The side tables are carved with eagles, and have marble tops inlaid with mosaics excavated from the Villa Adriana at Tivoli.

It is interesting to compare this serious classicism with Hogarth's 'Breakfast Scene'. Hogarth was no admirer of the Palladian movement, nor of the expensive taste for imported Italian paintings: the foreign arts of the past engaged those who, he thought, should rather patronize living English artists. Accordingly, he burlesqued the neo-Palladian grandeur of such houses as Holkham. On his walls hang paintings of saints who are quite incongruous with the dissipated life of the house. Next to these, an Italian mythological picture is so shocking that it has to be hidden by a curtain. Over the fireplace Cupid plays the bagpipes; the treasured Roman bust is hideous with wig and broken nose, and is surrounded by an assortment of oriental absurdities. Finally, Hogarth burlesqued the taste for exotic carved furniture in the wall clock. This piece he showed carved as a grove of trees containing a Chinese figure, a cat and two fish.

3 William Kent (?) (1685–1748). Settee. Victoria and Albert Museum, London.
   The settee is of painted and gilded pinewood. Although its origin
is unknown, it was almost certainly designed by William Kent around 1735.
It is similar to one at Holkham. Kent was the first architect to make a practice
of designing furniture for his state rooms. In architecture, his declared intentions
were to restore correct classical taste as it had been revived in Italy by Palladio
and in England by Inigo Jones. When designing furniture, however, Kent found
no suitable models from antiquity. Instead, this settee shows that he was
original and inventive. The cusped scrolls that act as legs are typical of his
style; so are the draped fruits and the architectural key pattern that forms
the seat rail. The cresting is more original still, with cornucopias separated by
fruits. The scallop shells in this piece are small, but in some 'Kent' furniture
they may be considerably larger and more prominent. Kent's furniture is
certainly derived from decorations by Bernini, Cortona and Guarini, even
though the English Palladians were in theory opposed to the extravagant and
'licentious' baroque works.

4 Looking glass. Victoria and Albert Museum, London.
   The looking glass is of pine, finely carved and gilded. Its design is architectural – although the columns appear rather long and slender – and uses
various conventional classical mouldings. The base with its acanthus leaf
and female mask against a shell is typically neo-Palladian, even though in the
details the carver is showing more freedom with rococo tendencies: the central
cartouche is asymmetrical. This attractive piece is Irish, and was probably made
in Dublin by the firm of Booker, about 1760.

5 Matthias Lock (working c.1740–70). Side table. Temple Newsam, Yorkshire.
   This massive side table, made to a design by Lock of about 1740, shows how
skilfully a basically classical form could be ornamented. Side tables at this period
tended to be in the style of William Kent and contained much animated
carving, so that they became almost sculptor's work. The piece here, however,
has a restrained carved head of Hercules, and his lion skin is hung through
carved rings.

6 Carved mahogany card table (c.1740). Stourhead, Wiltshire.
   The folding card table is a functional piece, designed by a furniture-maker
(as opposed to an architect). The lower part expands with a 'concertina' action.
As with so much English furniture, its maker is unknown, but the design and
quality of carving demonstrate the excellent standards of London cabinet-
makers around 1740. San Domingo or 'Spanish' mahogany, of which this is
made, was imported around 1725–45. The wood is very heavy, dark and close-
grained, and is usually unsuitable for veneer. On the other hand, it is good for
skilful carving, and, as the wood acquired a polish, such work sometimes took
on the appearance of bronze.

4

5

6

9

7 William Vile (died 1767). Mahogany bookcase. Buckingham Palace, London.

William Vile became cabinet-maker to the Royal Household in 1761. This piece was made for Queen Charlotte in 1762, and illustrates Vile's fine sense of design, impeccable taste and craftsmanship. The bookcase is architectural, and Palladian in form, but the style of carving is less severe than in the days of William Kent. The *appliqué* to the lower doors, and the frieze above the columns are influenced by the light touch of rococo, which by then had permeated the work of the craftsmen of St Martin's Lane. The large plate-glass panels in the doors and the virtual absence of glazing bars allow a clear view of the contents.

8 Thomas Chippendale (1718–1779). Carved mahogany wardrobe. Nostell Priory, Yorkshire.

Each large panel to the doors of this piece is veneered with a single sheet of wood, the patterns matched so that one reflects the other. The double serpentine front is shaped like a cupid's bow. Chippendale's wardrobe is a magnificent example of a utilitarian piece of furniture: the ornament consists chiefly in mouldings and carved scrolls and husks at the angles, while within it there are seven sliding shelves for clothes, all still covered with the original marbled paper. The wardrobe was made in 1766 and cost £37.

9 Thomas Chippendale. Library table. Nostell Priory, Yorkshire.

This piece was completed in 1766, and cost £72 10s. In its proportions and use of classical console scrolls with carved lion heads and feet, the table is in the Palladian tradition, but it shows the advance towards neoclassicism in the husk festoons. The panels outlined on each end and on the central drawers are of the pattern that had been used in French decoration since the sixteenth century. There are two drawers (one each side) and four cupboards. On one side the cupboards contain drawers, and on the other racks for folios. The whole is of Cuba mahogany, carved or veneered; originally the top was covered in black leather.

10 Looking glass (*c.*1760). Victoria and Albert Museum, London.

The pier glass, of carved, gilded pine, is one of many works of fine quality with no known maker. It closely resembles a pair at Woburn Abbey in Bedfordshire that are believed to be the work of Samuel Norman. Although this piece uses the acanthus and shells in Palladian tradition, there are small asymmetrical details that hint significantly at the rococo. The female busts are a motif often to be seen on French furniture, but here they are turned into sirens, with wings and rather uncomfortably attached fish tails.

10

11 Dining chair (*c.*1765–70). Victoria and Albert Museum, London.

The dining chair shown here is large and sturdy. The back, although made of solid mahogany, is cleverly veneered so that the grain runs perpendicular to the interlacing straps. The pattern of the back may owe something to the designs of de la Cour, a French engraver who worked in England between 1741 and 1747, and is also reminiscent of designs by Darly and Manwaring. The crisp acanthus and shellwork carving is restrained and unobtrusive, and the simple, clearly defined key-pattern is reminiscent of William Kent. The seat is covered with a hard-wearing fabric composed of horsehair that was much used in the eighteenth century and is still made in Somerset today.

12 Carved armchair (*c.*1760–5). (By courtesy of Mallett & Son, Bond Street, London.)

This detail shows how light decorative carving could be subordinate to straight lines and square joinery. Garlands of natural flowers are set in relief over an incised trellis. The open scrolled brackets are too delicate to be of much use for strengthening the joinery, but they soften the square lines. This chair, dating from the early 1760s, belongs to a large set originally made for St Giles's House in Dorset, for which Chippendale is thought to have supplied most of the furniture.

13 Mahogany stool (*c.*1755). Victoria and Albert Museum, London.

This is an example of the virtuosity of the London carvers. In mahogany 'every line and mark of the chisel' remains with crispness and vitality, and the finest chair-makers exercised their talents well on their demanding material. The seat rails have lively acanthus leaves flowing around central cartouches. The dolphin leg was illustrated on a 'French chair' in the first edition of Chippendale's *Director* (1754). A chair in the same museum has the arm supports also carved as dolphins.

14

15

16

19 Carved mahogany candlestand (*c.*1760). Victoria and Albert Museum, London.

A candlestand or *torchère* was a necessity for any room that was used after dark. This, one of a pair standing just over four and a half feet high, is rather taller than was usual. It shows the ease with which the Georgian joiner-carver could make a really graceful design and skilfully decorate it with carving. The raised gallery to the platform is a modern replacement. Chippendale illustrated several similar pieces in the *Director*, which show a greater display of carving.

14 Ribband-back chair. Victoria and Albert Museum, London,

Several examples of these ingenious chairs · have survived, which closely follow the pattern in the *Director* (see 15). The carving on the back is extremely fine, and the simulated ribbands are delicate even when carried out in hard mahogany.

15 Two ribband-back chairs. From Chippendale's *Director* (1754).

Chippendale himself claimed to have designed these chairs, and wrote in self-appreciation of these two designs: '[These], if I may speak without vanity, are the best I have ever seen (or perhaps have ever been made). The chair on the left hand has been executed from this design, which had an excellent effect, and gave satisfaction to all who saw it. I make no doubt but the other . . . will give the same content if properly handled in execution.' The chair seats were to be 16 inches high, $22\frac{3}{4}$ inches wide and 18 inches deep.

16 Mahogany dining chair (*c.*1755). Victoria and Albert Museum, London.

The chair back closely follows one of Chippendale's designs of 1754. However, it is unlikely that the chair was made in the Chippendale workshop, for the cabriole leg, with stiff acanthus carving and a pad foot, is of an earlier type that had been fashionable 25 years earlier. The seats of dining chairs were usually covered with red morocco.

17 Rectangular mahogany tea table (*c.*1750). Victoria and Albert Museum, London.

Sometimes called silver tables, these were to hold the silver tea tray and the porcelain cups and saucers. The fragility of the laminated fret gallery is characteristic of such tables, and is proof of the care taken over the tea ceremony, when the hostess would preside over the refreshment and conversation of the company. The piece still retains the cabriole leg with claw-and-ball foot, which had been introduced about 1710. By 1754 the claw-and-ball was old-fashioned, and Chippendale did not illustrate it in the *Director*.

18 Mahogany tea kettle stand (*c.*1755). Victoria and Albert Museum, London.

At tea, which was normally drunk after dinner, the kettle or hot water urn was placed on a stand, made specifically for the purpose. The rail of the gallery has an inlaid strip of brass. Tea kettle stands, especially when finely carved, are valuable collectors' pieces today. Tripod stands were in use about 1730, and can be seen in conversation pictures by Hogarth and other artists. Sometimes they have a slide at one side intended to hold the tea pot as it was being refilled.

17
18

19

25

20 The picture gallery. Corsham Court, Wiltshire.

The gallery was designed in 1757 by the architect Lancelot Brown (better known as the landscape gardener 'Capability' Brown who revolutionized the appearance of the English park), in order to house the picture collection made by Sir Paul Methuen (1682–1757). Italian paintings by such masters as Carracci, Guido Reni and Salvator Rosa form the basis of this collection, and are hung beside Rubens and Van Dyck. A suite of smaller state rooms containing smaller pictures, and cabinets and other curios from Italy, lead from the gallery.

The gallery itself is of satisfying proportions, being in fact a triple cube, 24 by 72 by 24 feet. The ceiling was designed by Brown and carried out by the Bristol plasterer, Thomas Stocking. The fireplace is the work of the popular immigrant sculptor Peter Scheemakers, and on it stands a bust of Sir Paul Methuen. The modern Spanish carpet was designed by the present Lord Methuen and its pattern reflects the ceiling.

By eighteenth-century standards this picture gallery was amply furnished. There are pier glasses between the windows, with marble-topped tables below that hold glass lustres and candelabra. There are large Chinese porcelain vases of the K'ang 'Hsi and earlier periods in blue and white and in polychrome, Japanese Imari jars, and four chests made of Chinese lacquer panels. Finally, there is the large and important set of seat furniture, comprising thirty armchairs, four settees, two stools and eight window seats. These stood round the walls, leaving the centre of the room bare (some are in adjoining rooms). The walls, as well as the chairs, are still covered in the original crimson silk damask that was bought in 1765–9.

21, 22 Mahogany sofa and detail. Picture gallery, Corsham Court, Wiltshire.

Like its counterparts in the state rooms of France and Italy, such seat furniture was chiefly for display purposes. These chairs and sofas are large but simple in design, and form an integral part of the architecture of the room (see 20). Ornament on this furniture is confined to brackets suggesting acanthus fronds, narrow rope and gadroon mouldings, and rosettes; even the stretchers are plain and functional. The brass nails securing the original upholstery are interesting, for they show how 'close nailing' became an essential part of the design and decoration, and how, by a gentle curve at the angles below the arms, the nailing helped to resolve an otherwise uncomfortable junction.

23 Mahogany pole screen (*c.*1765). Victoria and Albert Museum, London.

This anonymous piece has a base not unlike the designs of Chippendale's published patterns: its structure relies on a simple arrangement of C-scrolls which was within 'the capacity of every Workman'. At the head of each curved leg there is a sunk panel with gothic trefoil cusping. The needlework panel is of a charming Dutch-inspired design and might be a little earlier than the mahogany base. Just such a screen is seen at the extreme right of Hogarth's painting (plate 1).

24 Thomas Chippendale. Mahogany stool. Christ Church College, Oxford.

This stool is one of a set of twelve supplied for the new library at Christ Church in 1764. The total bill (£38 15s) does not seem excessive nor does the 18s 6d charged for their carriage from London. The stools were clearly intended for decoration rather than for use. Like the furniture at Corsham Court (shown opposite), they represent the traditionally simple taste of the Englishman. Made from dark mahogany, they are of an attractive arched shape with generously curved supports, and are not like any of the patterns shown in the *Director*. The prominent central rosette is a neoclassical touch that Chippendale probably learnt from Adam (see 50), and it is set above what is a mere ghost of the rococo leaf.

23   24

25 James Paine (*c.*1716–1789). The state bedroom, Nostell Priory, Yorkshire.

Paine's architecture was generally of Palladian character, but he had studied drawing in the St Martin's Lane Academy, probably under Gravelot. In 1754 Paine built himself a house in St Martin's Lane, close to Chippendale's premises. This plaster ceiling of the 1740s clearly shows his early affection for the rococo. The doorcase and chimneypiece are Palladian in structure but rococo in ornament.

At a later date, 1771, Chippendale provided and hung the Chinese wallpaper and supplied the green and gold japanned furniture (see 38).

26 Matthias Lock (working *c.*1740–70). Side table and pier glass. Victoria and Albert Museum, London.

The early rococo side table and mirror frame, of about 1745, may appear overloaded with ornament and rather Germanic in taste. Yet basically their design has the same harmony of proportion and balance to be seen in Lock's earlier side table (see 5). Lock had a clearer understanding of rococo principles than any other English designer. His original sketches for these pieces survive, and include information about the work involved. It took 89 days to make the table, and Lock himself worked on it for 15 days. The mirror frame took 138 days, Lock giving it 20 days. Originally these pieces were probably gilded all over. Looking glass plates were enormously expensive, and could cost nearly £100. The table top is veneered with onyx.

27, 28 Mahogany commode and detail. Private Collection.

This elaborate piece is similar to a 'French commode table' in the *Director*. It is chiefly by such exaggerated rococo patterns (and those with Chinese or gothic alternatives) that the 'Chippendale' style is recognized today. Full-blown rococo commodes are rare in England, and as in France were principally show pieces for the formal saloon or drawing room. The scroll and shell-work are carved in solid mahogany, and the top and drawer fronts are veneered in figured wood. The carving has a curious Germanic character, particularly in the manner in which the legs join the body. The handles could have been designed for a different piece.

26

27   28

25

29

30

29 Painted pine chimneypiece and overmantel (*c.*1750). Victoria and Albert Museum, London.

Pine is softer than mahogany, and lends itself to virtuoso carving. This piece is typical of 'St Martin's Lane rococo'. Yet it remains disciplined and logical, and the underlying sense of structure and proportion is almost classical. This, perhaps, is why Chippendale prefaced his *Director* with detailed measurements of the five classical orders, saying that they were the 'very soul and basis' of the cabinet-maker's art.

The fire basket and fender are of steel.

30 Armchair (*c.*1760–5). Victoria and Albert Museum, London.

This piece is carved out of solid mahogany, and closely follows a design dated 1759 in the *Director* (third edition) for a 'French chair'. 'French' referred to the comfortable upholstery of back, seat and arms, and to the rococo-style carving. Chippendale wrote of these chairs: 'Sometimes the dimensions vary according to the Bigness of the rooms they are intended for. A skilful workman may also lessen the carving without any Prejudice to the design. Both the backs and seats must be covered with tapestry, or other sort of needlework.' Such a chair as this is unlikely to be confused with one made in France, for solid mahogany was not used in that country before the 1780s. Nor do the contours flow as smoothly as they would in a Louis XV chair.

31 Gilded looking glass (*c*.1765). Victoria and Albert Museum, London.

This mirror is thought to have been designed by Thomas Chippendale, and may have been one of two supplied to the Duke of Portland in 1766. It is a good example of the work of the London carver-gilders during the 1760s, who by then were seduced by the almost limitless possibilities of carving in pine. The lower part includes candlebranches.

32 Thomas Johnson (working *c*.1755–61). One of a pair of looking glasses. Corsham Court, Wiltshire.

The mirror illustrated is decorated with feathered birds, oak leaves and twigs, all suspended by a fine simulated knotted cord. Johnson was a virtuoso carver in wood. The work on these mirror frames is attributed to him because they follow one of his engraved designs, published in 1758.

33 Thomas Johnson. Designs for tables. From the *Collection of Designs* (1758).

As a rococo designer, Thomas Johnson went to further extremes than any other in London. His *girandoles* show little landscapes with columns, rocks, water, animals and human beings all engaged in some action. They are often in the Chinese manner, but may also be classical (with ruins), or rustic (with windmills). The central table in this plate contains an illustration to Aesop's fable 'The Fox and the Cat', taken from Francis Barlow's engraving of 1687.

34 John Linnell (*c.*1737–1796). Pier glass. Dyrham Park, Gloucestershire.

The pier glass and the oval overmantel reflected in it are very similar to a number of Linnell's drawings of about 1760 that are preserved in the Victoria and Albert Museum. Linnell evidently learnt rococo principles at St Martin's Lane Academy: his mirrors are in his own personal style, and are more refined and sinuous than those of Chippendale or Johnson. The large plate is framed by straight lines and long thin scrolls of moulded wood, which form the basis of the structure; the acanthus leaves and trailing flowers are applied in *papier mâché*. The console table may also have been supplied by Linnell, but is in the later neoclassical style (see 64).

35 William Linnell (*c.*1708–1763). State bed in the Chinese style. Victoria and Albert Museum, London.

This was part of a suite of furniture made about 1754 for the Chinese bedroom at Badminton House, Gloucestershire. The remainder included chairs, china shelves, and a commode (see 36). Recently it has been shown that these pieces should be attributed to William Linnell's firm in Berkeley Square. The bed is japanned in red, black and gilt with Chinese motifs. The canopy is derived from a Chinese pavilion or temple. The hangings are modern.

36 William Linnell. Japanned dressing commode. Victoria and Albert Museum, London.

This belongs to the Badminton Chinese bedroom (see 35). It shows how Chinese paling, frets and decoration could be grafted on to furniture which otherwise remained quite English. The lattice doors are an unusual feature. The japanning closely imitates Chinese lacquer screens.

37 China cabinet. (By courtesy of Mallett & Son, Bond Street, London.)

This is an unusually fine example of a china cabinet in the chinoiserie style. All the carved details are gilded: the supports are carved with rocks and palm trees, and the upper part has three pavilion roofs. The other carving is a typically English mixture of classical, rococo and naturalistic, and the result is certainly exotic. The maker is not known.

35
36

38 Thomas Chippendale. Furniture in the state bedroom, Nostell Priory, Yorkshire.

The bedroom suite at Nostell was japanned green and gold. Chippendale himself supplied and hung the imported wallpaper in 1771, and the accounts for the furniture are dated the same year. The pier glass is in chinoiserie, with a temple and exotic birds as cresting. But bamboos and peonies seem to have been too difficult for English designers, and were replaced by acanthus, laurel and roses. The design includes regular rococo scrollwork. It cost £68.

Fourteen 'India arm'd chairs' were supplied at 2½ guineas each. The commode, fitted with twelve drawers behind three doors, cost £15 10s. These had unmistakably neoclassical supports (see 50).

39 Mahogany chair. Victoria and Albert Museum, London.

The open Chinese lattice back is based on an illustration in the first edition of the *Director*. Chippendale wrote (in 1754) that the Chinese manner had 'never yet arrived to any perfection . . . (but) admits the greatest variety'. In the third edition (1762) he said that such chairs 'are very proper for a Lady's Dressing Room: especially if it is hung with India paper'. The frets on the legs and stretchers and other carved details appear more European than Chinese.

40 Breakfast table. Victoria and Albert Museum, London.

An identical piece was illustrated in the first edition of Chippendale's *Director* (1754). It was an advance on the simple tripod table (see 1), for it provided two flaps, a drawer and a protected cupboard below. Such pieces had many uses, and later developed into the Pembroke table (see 81).

41 James Wyatt (1746–1813). The 'strawberry room' from Lee Priory, Kent. Victoria and Albert Museum, London.

The room was designed about 1785 as a small study, and the mirrored doors enclose bookshelves. It is in the same dilettante mood as Horace Walpole's Strawberry Hill, from which it takes its name. The gothic chairs of mahogany, about 1770, are more advanced than any patterns in the *Director*, and their backs show a closer observation of medieval tracery in windows and screens.

39

40

41

42 Side table and mirror. The Vyne, Hampshire.

These were probably made about 1755, although they are more gothic in their details than most furniture of the period, their design still includes rococo C-scrolls. They are made of pine, gilded and ebonized, and are set against original wall covering of Italian flowered silk damask.

43 Mahogany sideboard table (*c*.1755). Victoria and Albert Museum, London.

Based on a design in the first edition of the *Director* (1754), this table has simplified gothic details in the pinced feet, the bows in the open supports, and the blind fret in the frieze. On comparing the fret with that in plate 39, it is evident that Gothic and Chinese patterns were easily confused.

The clock is of ebony and gilt metal (*c*.1760).

44 Thomas Chippendale. Design for bookcase. From the *Director* (third edition), 1762.

Chippendale's gothic made use of pointed arches, cusps, quatrefoils, pinnacles and crockets, and the ever-popular cluster columns. These motifs combine attractively with the very un-gothic glazing bars to the upper doors. Gothic, being a literary study, was particularly suitable for libraries and bookcases.

42

43

44

45 James Stuart (1713–1788). Design for the painted room at Spencer House. British Museum, London.

Stuart was the pioneer designer of neoclassical interiors in England; this room, dated 1759 on the drawing, was among the first to be completed. The pilasters have Vitruvian scrolls (taken from the Arch of the Silversmiths in Rome), and the walls are in the tradition of Raphael's grotesques in the Vatican. But there are also memories of Pompeian decorations that had been discovered near Naples since 1738.

The little group of furniture in the drawing is also an early manifestation of neoclassicism. The table with its straight fluted frieze and tapering legs is fully neoclassical, even though the carved lion beneath it seems to have survived from the sculptured furniture of William Kent. On the table is a small tripod candelabrum. This pattern, probably Stuart's invention, also became an international form, and in France was known as an *athénienne* (see 72).

46 Robert Adam (1728–1792) and Thomas Chippendale. Gilded armchair. Victoria and Albert Museum, London.

This armchair was designed by Robert Adam in 1764, and executed by Chippendale, who described it in his account as 'exceedingly richly carved in the Antick manner'. The vigorously carved ornaments include touches of neoclassical decoration in the honeysuckle, sphinxes and foliage scrolls. At this time, however, Adam had not yet fully developed his neoclassical style in respect of furniture, and the chair remains of the familiar baroque type called 'French' in the *Director*. The shells and lion feet also derive from the earlier period.

46

47

48

49

50

51

52

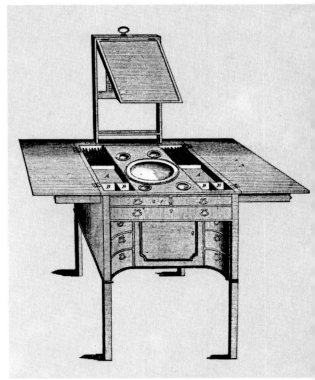

47 Robert Adam. Lyre-back dining chair. Osterley Park, Middlesex.

This is one of a set of ten dining chairs. Adam's drawing for these is undated, but they appear to have been made in 1767. most probably by John Linnell. They are extremely graceful, showing the hand of a true artist. About fifteen years later the lyre-back on chairs became popular in France and Italy.

48 Thomas Chippendale. Library chair. Nostell Priory, Yorkshire.

In 1768 Chippendale supplied this set of six chairs with lyre-backs, and 'the carving exceedingly rich in the antique taste'. It seems that he was imitating Adam's design (see 47), but it may be unfair to compare these two sets because Chippendale's fine work then appears rather heavy. The blocks, square or round at the cap and foot of the leg are characteristic of Chippendale's designs. Originally the seats were covered in green horsehair cloth, and each chair cost £6.

49 Thomas Chippendale. Upholstered chair. (By courtesy of Mallett & Son, Bond Street, London.)

This chair, probably made before 1770, has a French-style rococo frame ornamented with neoclassical fluting, husk festoons and honeysuckle. It is identical with a famous set made for Harewood House, and probably originated there.

50 Thomas Chippendale. Hall chair. Harewood House, Yorkshire.

This hall chair of painted pine was designed for Harewood House about 1770, and shows how thoroughly Chippendale had absorbed the neoclassical principles established by Adam.

51 Thomas Chippendale. Dressing table. Nostell Priory, Yorkshire.

This table, made in 1769, is of much the same design as plate 53, but is neoclassical in its flutings and small medallions. It has a fine mahogany veneer and the compartments hold silver fittings. It cost £12 10s.

52 Thomas Chippendale. Wall barometer. Nostell Priory, Yorkshire.

This is veneered with tulipwood and ebony with carved and gilded ornaments, and was made in 1769. The honeysuckle cresting was frequently used by Chippendale at this period, and without doubt he had taken it from Adam, as well as the trailing husks and rams' heads. The works are by the Swiss clockmaker Justin Vuilliamy. The three stages of the case are differentiated by columns, satyr herm busts and scrolls, all of which seem to be copied from some Italian sixteenth-century cabinet; their workmanship is very fine, making the gilt cresting and pendant appear slightly cumbersome.

53

53 Thomas Chippendale. Design for shaving table from the *Director* (third edition), 1762.

The lines of this useful piece of furniture are simple and functional. It has a rising mirror, but the lower part has a recess for knees, indicating that when closed it may serve as a writing table.

54, 55 Thomas Chippendale. Library table (and detail). Leeds City Art Gallery, Temple Newsam House, Yorkshire.

This, made for Harewood House in Yorkshire, about 1770, is probably the most famous single piece of furniture in England. Chippendale's marquetry furniture for Harewood (shown on these pages and in plates 59 and 87) is superb. As Oliver Brackett said: 'he strained every nerve and muscle to excel', and it bears comparison with the products of the best cabinet-makers of France. The designs are considered no longer to have come from Adam, but to be Chippendale's own inventions.

The library table may be compared with that recently delivered to Nostell (see 9). Each pedestal contains a cupboard with drawers. The panels are veneered with rosewood and tulipwood banding, inlaid with freely classical urns and foliage, and a *guilloche* frieze (a decoration of intersecting curved lines). The veneer appears to have been bleached at some time, for the rosewood interior is of a rich purple-brown (also found on other Chippendale pieces at Harewood). The ormolu mounts remain, at present, anonymous.

56, 57 Thomas Chippendale. Secretaire and detail. Harewood House, Yorkshire.

This is a small example, only four and a half feet high, of the upright type of secretaire that was becoming common in France and Italy, but is rare in England at this period. The ground is of satinwood banded with tulipwood; the medallions are of amaranth, and the marquetry is of ebony and fruitwoods (partly stained green or shaded).

58 Dressing commode. Harewood House, Yorkshire.

This commode is veneered with a strongly figured satinwood with tulipwood crossbanding; the inlaid foliage is of stained fruitwood. It has two medallions in the Pompeian style of Minerva and Diana, partly inlaid with ivory and ebony. This masterpiece of English cabinet work was finished in 1773 and cost £86.

56

57

58

59

59 Thomas Chippendale. Side table. Harewood House, Yorkshire.

This is one of many with carved gilt legs and marquetry top, and is based on the rectilinear style of James Stuart and Robert Adam, although it shows the features of Chippendale's personal style. The sturdy legs with their exaggerated feet and block capitals have French antecedents, and the rather heavily carved husk festoons are like those on the Nostell barometer (see 52). The top has a leaf and medallion pattern inlaid in stained fruitwoods on a rosewood ground. The rosewood appears to be its original unfaded purple-brown colour, which was then briefly in fashion, and has not been bleached as it presumably was on the library table (see 54). The tulipwood crossbanding glows pink.

60, 61 John Cobb (working c.1755–78). Marquetry commode and pedestals. Robert Adam pier glass. Corsham Court, Wiltshire.

These certainly have French ancestry, even if their shapes have moved far away from their original type. The Louis XV *bombé* (convex) form remains, but the marquetry decoration is almost entirely neoclassical, with oval medallions, husks and honeysuckle. The marquetry vases of flowers seem to be of French derivation, and the same may be said of the ormolu corner mounts. If the pedestals were ever intended as candlestands they soon lost this function. The platforms seem too small to be of practical use, and mounted marble urns were fixed to them within ten years. The furniture was made around 1772. John Cobb had been partner to William Vile since about 1755.

Elaborate marquetry had been out of fashion since 1700, and its sudden revival in English furniture in the 1760s seems to have occurred when commerce was revived between England and France at the end of the war in 1763. The smooth surfaces of neoclassical furniture lent themselves well to such decoration. A competent French maker, Pierre Langlois, who established himself in London about 1760, made several commodes of the French *bombé* form for English patrons. These pieces have tops of wood (rather than of marble as was the custom in France); generally they are covered in rich floral inlay and have elaborate ormolu handles and corner mounts. It may well have been competition from Langlois that inspired Chippendale, Cobb and others to return to the field of marquetry.

The large pier glass (see 60) was designed by Robert Adam himself, and supplied in 1772, although in style it seems rather earlier. At Corsham a number of the best London architects and craftsmen were employed, but the actual maker of this piece is not recorded.

62

62 Robert Adam. Library. Osterley Park, Middlesex.

This room, designed in 1766, is transitional between Adam's early period and his maturity. The Vitruvian bookcases and framed paintings by Antonio Zucchi are an intrinsic part of the room decoration. In the ceiling there are what Adam described as 'a beautiful variety of light mouldings, gracefully formed, delicately enriched and arranged with propriety and skill' (see 66). These, derived from his knowledge of Roman stucco work, were certainly one of Adam's most important innovations, and replaced the 'ponderous compartment ceiling' that had been in consistent use by the English Palladian school.

The personal achievement of Robert Adam is as important in furniture as it is in architecture. In France and Italy, between 1754 and 1758, Adam made the acquaintance of *avant-garde* artists who were then formulating the principles of neoclassicism. Adam studied at Rome, Naples, and Spalato; he learnt the necessary art of drawing from the Frenchman Clérisseau and became a friend of Piranesi; by maintaining his international contacts he remained for several years in the forefront of the neoclassical movement. A very short time after he returned to England, he had obtained a large number of commissions, chiefly to redesign interiors of country houses. He gained the reputation of being fastidious with his work, taking immense pains to correct every detail. Adam treated the Vitruvian orders in a cavalier fashion, and the result, although artistic and decorative, is not academic. Towards the end of the 1770s he was heavily criticized by many of his former champions, who were tired of 'gingerbread and snippets of embroidery', and wished their interior decorations to be in the more correct and serious spirit of antiquity.

63 John Linnell. Chair and writing table. Osterley Park, Middlesex.

When the library at Osterley was completed in 1773, John Linnell designed eight chairs, two writing tables and a pedestal library table. They are veneered with rosewood, and the splats and inlaid 'wave' motifs are in satinwood set against sycamore panels; the festoons hung on the legs are in gilt metal. For these chairs Linnell simplified the lyre-back, which originally had been Adam's invention. These pieces do not have the massive quality of early French neoclassical furniture, but they do follow the same rectangular lines, prominent Vitruvian wave friezes and draped festoons associated with that French style. There may be a distant relationship between this furniture and the first piece of neoclassical furniture known, the famous *bureau plat 'à la grecque'* of 1757, now in the Château de Chantilly.

64 Robert Adam. *Girandole*. Osterley Park, Middlesex.

The *girandole* was a purely ornamental piece, intended to provide candlebrackets against a reflecting background. This example was designed for the long gallery at Osterley by Adam in 1770, and a set of six were carried out, probably by John Linnell, with some alterations. It is of a refined and delicate composition, even if the mermaids rather lack repose, through being set in oblique lines. The result, with the females limply holding festoons, and the complicated shapes of the festoons, is in some respects more typical of Linnell's style than of Adam's.

65 John Linnell. Design for an overmantel. Victoria and Albert Museum.

This design, one of a large number of drawings that were fortunately preserved after Linnell's death, is dated 1773; but the other existing drawings show that Linnell was interested in neoclassical details at least ten years earlier. It is not hard to recognize here the same hand that had designed the rococo mantel for Dyrham (see 34).

64

63

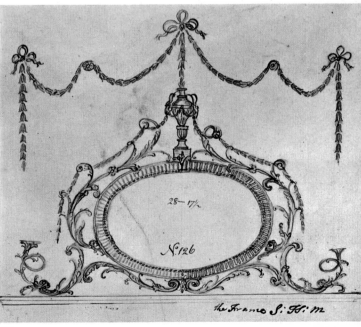

65

66

66 Robert Adam and (?) John Linnell. Sideboard table and urns. Osterley Park, Middlesex.

A drawing by Robert Adam exists for this sideboard table, and is dated 1767. It was probably executed by Linnell, and is remarkable in its complicated baluster legs, whose lotus capitals support blocks set below the finely carved frieze. Such delicacy of detail can be seen in French furniture of about ten years later. The base of this table is in gilded softwood, while the top is of finely coloured mahogany, enriched by a carved and gilded *guilloche* along the edge.

The accompanying pedestals with urns, probably also by Adam and Linnell, are carved, painted white and gilt, and the handles are of gilt brass. They are based on ancient Roman pedestal altars, and the upper parts are stylized amphoras. Adam was the first to combine these antique shapes and make out of them the sideboard suite for the dining room. The urns are lined with lead to hold water, and the pedestals form cupboards.

67 Robert Adam. Design for a ceiling to a music room.

This shows a typical design of Adam's mature period. It was for the music room in 20 St James's Square, London, designed 1766–72, and published in the *Works in Architecture of Robert and James Adam* (vol II, 1777). All the plaster-work was executed in very low relief. The repertory of forms is limited chiefly to husks, slender acanthus scrolls, honeysuckle and urns; there are also delicate musical trophies supported by drapery. Everything was picked out in contrasting, but carefully chosen, colourings that never obtrude or jar. The colouring in this engraved design is Adam's own, for in each book he coloured a few plates in order to leave a true record for posterity.

68 Robert Adam. Marquetry commode. Osterley House, Middlesex.

This commode was one of a pair designed by Adam and probably made by Linnell, with beautiful marquetry pictures of Diana, Flora and Pomona. The matching commode shows Venus between two dancing girls. There seems to be no iconographical significance for the figure subjects. The little bust relief in the frieze is of the heathen Antinous, where the companion piece has Fiammingo's St Susanna. The body of the commode is veneered in the then popular hardwood or stained sycamore, and the frieze is of satinwood. The ornaments are inlaid in natural and stained woods, and applied gilt bronze. This simple, almost semicircular shape is typical of Adam and remained popular up to about 1790.

67

68

69, 70 Robert Adam and (?) Thomas Chippendale. Side table and marble top. Nostell Priory, Yorkshire.

Adam's drawing for the pair of side tables for Nostell Priory is dated 1775. They were probably made by Chippendale, but no document remains to prove this. The design looks somewhat fragile, with the legs breaking into oval medallions, unusually long husk festoons, and curved stretchers supporting an urn. This is not altogether typical of English furniture, and clearly during his middle period Adam was still trying to keep abreast of French and Italian styles. The marble top shows his more familiar geometrical patterns, and the design is inlaid in coloured *scagliola* (imitation stone made of cement and chips), in a technique that was known as 'Bossi work'.

71 Robert Adam. The tapestry room. Osterley Park, Middlesex.

This is one of the most highly coloured of all Adam's interiors. It is not large, but crowded with incidents. The predominating colour is the deep rose damask ground of the tapestry walls and chair covers; the ceiling has a contrasting duck-egg blue ground, and the simulated gold on the tapestry borders and the gilded details of the chairs and ceiling lend brilliance to the ensemble. The room is a complete unity: Adam designed the ceiling, fireplace, doors, pedestals, and the carpet, made at the Moorfields factory in London, which echoes the design of the ceiling. Nearly every feature in the room is set with coloured medallions, large or small.

The tapestries are French, dated 1775, and have scenes from 'Les Amours des Dieux' by Boucher. Designed in 1757 at the Gobelins factory, Paris, six sets were imported for particular English houses. The Gobelins also supplied the chair covers and, it seems, a sketch for making the medallion-back chairs. No drawing for them by Adam is known, and the round seats are in any case a French feature.

72   73

74

72 Robert Adam. Pedestal. Osterley Park, Middlesex.

Adam's designs were not usually as complicated as in this piece; his geometrical outlines were generally simple and clearly defined. Although the overall effect is very sophisticated, much of the ornament lacks a proper structural purpose, and appears contrived and affected. Two platforms at the base seem unnecessarily affected, and the urn, though beautiful, has no architectural justification.

73 Robert Adam. Painted pine pedestal. Victoria and Albert Museum, London.

The pedestal was designed by Adam about 1770 and has almost as much carved decoration as plate 72; but this, by contrast, is an example of clarity. The base is probably derived from an ancient marble candelabrum in the Vatican. The upper part is a tripod stand that became known as an *athénienne*, and could serve many purposes. The blue and ivory colouring is original.

74 Robert Adam. Design for a medallion-back chair. Sir John Soane's Museum, London.

This design is dated 1779. The patterns on the back and seat were usually painted on white satin.

75 Robert Adam. Medallion-back chair. Osterley Park, Middlesex.

These bedroom chairs were made to an Adam design of 1777. They are related to Louis XVI chairs but their frames are slender, and there is English refinement in the carved decoration.

76 Robert Adam. Bed. Osterley Park, Middlesex.

The bed, one of Adam's most elaborate designs, has painted satinwood posts, a gilded canopy and dome, and dark green velvet curtains embroidered with flowers and heraldic devices. The interior and the walls are hung in pale green silk. In 1778, Horace Walpole found it 'too theatric, like a modern headdress'.

77 Robert Adam. 'Etruscan' chairs and frieze. Osterley Park, Middlesex.

Designed in 1776, Adam's so-called 'Etruscan' style was based on the Greek vases which were then eagerly collected by Englishmen; but the pale blue ground was never found on ancient vases. These chairs, of painted beech with cane seats and loose cushions, are of an economical pattern, and in their appearance anticipate the Sheraton period of the 1790s.

78 Bookcase. Leeds City Art Gallery, Temple Newsam, Yorkshire.
The bookcase, one of a pair, is a striking piece, made in cherrywood with mahogany banding. With its linear glazing bars and gadroon mouldings it is in the Hepplewhite style of about 1780, which never went completely out of production in the nineteenth century.

79 George Hepplewhite (died 1786). Design for secretaire-bookcase.
This engraving appears in Hepplewhite's *Cabinet-Maker and Upholsterer's Guide* published by his widow Alice in 1788, and is a useful and agreeable piece, in accordance with the *Guide*'s opening sentence: 'To unite elegance and utility, and blend the useful with the agreeable, has ever been considered a difficult, but an honourable task.' Many such pieces survive today, with more or less decoration; almost always the glass in the doors was divided by thin shaped glazing bars, either geometrical, or outlining classical shapes such as urns or drapery. The secretaire drawer was considered more elegant than the sloping front of a bureau.

80 Three types of open-back chair. Victoria and Albert Museum, London.
All these three types of chair were made in great quantities with innumerable variations in design, materials and quality. The oval-back (left), derived from the medallion-back, was already going out of fashion by 1790, but the shield-back remained popular for much longer, and Sheraton illustrated several examples. The one shown (right) is of painted satinwood, and was probably made by George Seddon. The centre chair was illustrated in the third edition of the *Guide* (1794). Rectangular shapes became popular during the 1790s, and became very elaborate in Sheraton's designs.

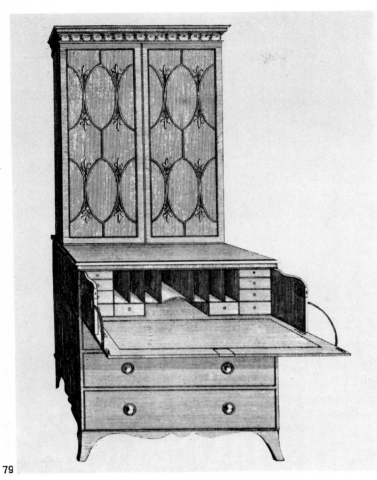

79

80

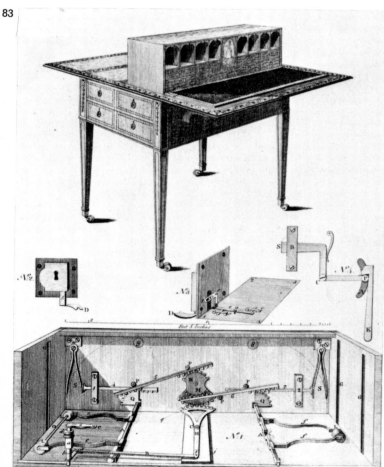

81 82

81 Inlaid satinwood Pembroke table. Victoria and Albert Museum, London.
 These were originally named after a certain Countess of Pembroke, and were described by Sheraton as 'a piece for a gentleman or lady to Breakfast upon'. This table (c.1790) has two flaps supported by hinged brackets and an oval top that is flattened at the corners, so that when the flaps are lowered the rails of the drawer are hidden. It is veneered in strongly figured satinwood, and inlaid with wreaths of naturalistic flowers.

82 Lady's writing cabinet. Victoria and Albert Museum, London.
 Sheraton illustrated many types of writing cabinet in his book, most of them delicate toys for scribbling notes. This example is light in colour, its satinwood has 'fiddle-back' figuring. The medallions are of yew and have finely inlaid borders. The stand has a drawer with a writing slide and fittings.

83 Thomas Sheraton (1751–1806). Design for a 'Harlequin' table.
 Basically this example is a Pembroke table converted to a writing table, with a rack of drawers and pigeonholes which rise from the table top, when released by a spring. Sheraton accounted for the name *Harlequin* by relating it to the Italian comedy, for, he said, 'in exhibitions of this sort there is generally a great deal of machinery in the scenery'.

84 Commode. Victoria and Albert Museum, London.
 The commode has a serpentine front, broken by upright stiles which continue the lines of the legs; its decoration of natural flowers shows some French influence. It is of satinwood and has simple inlaid lines in mahogany and other woods. The silvered handles and lock plates are reduced to a minimum.

85 Parlour chair. Dyrham Park, Gloucestershire.
 This is in the Sheraton style, one of a set made about 1795, painted white and gilded. The pierced splat is adapted from ancient bronze tripods. The round seat and the panelled top rail are of French origin, and the Pompeian *putti* on the top rail are in *grisaille* (painted in grey tints).

86 Thomas Sheraton. Design for a card table.
 Sheraton wrote 'the ornaments may be japanned on the frames and carved in the legs'. The French details are based on Paris fashions of the 1780s by makers such as Carlin and Weisweiler.

84

85   86

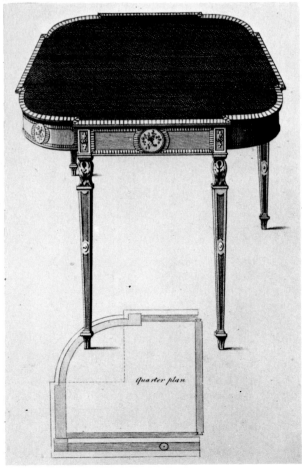

quarter plan

87

87 Thomas Chippendale. Sideboard table, pedestals and wine cooler. Harewood House, Yorkshire.

The sideboard suite was the invention of Robert Adam, who illustrated two examples in *The Works* (1772). In this example Chippendale imitated Adam (see 66). It is veneered with rosewood of a dark, almost purple colour; it has tulipwood banding and gilt bronze mounts, and was made about 1772.

The sideboard table is simple, containing no drawers, but the pedestals are full of different contrivances. One is lined with zinc, and contains metal racks for hot plates with a charcoal burner below. The other pedestal has two lead or zinc-lined drawers, one to cool bottles or glasses, and one fitted with a draining plug, where the glasses could be washed without taking them from the room. The urns are for hot water. They were often fitted with racks for cutlery.

88 Pair of mahogany dining tables. Victoria and Albert Museum, London.

This dining table, *c*.1775, had evolved from the old-fashioned gate-leg tables. It is in fact two tables with square flaps, that are clipped together. When not in use the table was placed in the corridor, or each end-piece, folded, stood against the wall as a pier table. The fluted frieze and tapering legs headed by medallions show the neoclassical influence of Robert Adam. By 1790 these tables were generally given semicircular end-pieces.

The other furniture in this plate has been illustrated elsewhere (73, 80, 84). The carpet is Axminster, *c*.1785.

89 Thomas Shearer (working *c*.1788). Designs for cellaret sideboards. From the *Book of Prices*, 1788.

The sideboard was an exclusively English invention, and was first illustrated by Hepplewhite and Shearer in 1788. There was considerable variation in shape, size and number of drawers or cupboards. At least two lined drawers were essential, one for holding bottles, and one for washing glasses. The central drawer was for cutlery. The sideboard was nearly always a large piece of furniture, so that silver could be well displayed on the top. The front had to be carefully shaped because a very long piece could easily become too deep at the centre to be convenient. Many sideboards have a small side cupboard for a chamber pot, because it was considered bad manners for gentlemen to leave the room during drinking sessions.

90 Thomas Sheraton. Designs for a Drawing and Writing Table, and for a Dining Parlour imitating that at Carlton House. Engraving dated 1793 from the *Drawing Book*.

This type has long been known as a 'Carlton House writing table'. It was first illustrated by Shearer in 1792. Sheraton said they were finished in mahogany or satinwood, with a brass rim round the upper part. A 'drawing table' was one which had a rising desk top, which Sheraton provided for here. Drawing was a most lady-like accomplishment as leisure increased.

The dining room at Carlton House was drawn from memory after 'a very transient view of it'. The near wall has been laid flat on the ground. The furniture, all mahogany, includes 'a large range of dining tables, standing on pillars with four claws each, which is now the fashionable way of making these tables. The chairs are made in the style of the French, with broad top-rails hanging over each back foot . . . the seats covered with red leather.' A sideboard stands at each end, through columns of *scagliola*, and lit up by wall lights. Sheraton omitted the French-style curtains.

88

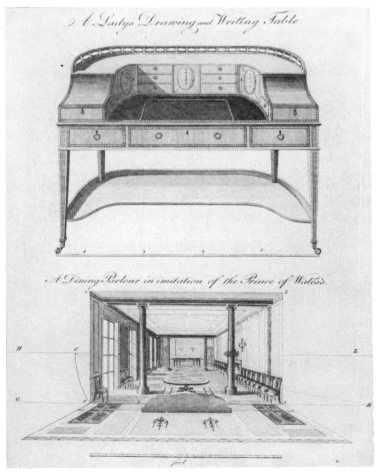

A Lady's Drawing and Writing Table.

A Dining Parlour in imitation of the Prince of Wales's.

89   90

91 Thomas Chippendale the younger (1749–1822). Armchair. Stourhead, Wiltshire.

Twelve of these chairs were delivered for the picture gallery at Stourhead in 1802. The influence of Sheraton is clearly apparent: the chairs have 'French' panelled backs and a severely economical outline. They are of satinwood, with ebony lines and mouldings, and caned seats that require cushions. The younger Chippendale's furniture of this period is excellent in both quality and design.

92 Thomas Chippendale the younger. Sofa table. Stourhead, Wiltshire.

The sofa table became fashionable towards 1800, and was a kind of extended Pembroke table, designed primarily to be placed before a sofa for needlework or informal meals. The pair at Stourhead are larger than was usual, and are made of a pale-coloured rosewood. The lyre-ends are probably of French derivation.

93 Library. Stourhead, Wiltshire.

The library, and also the picture-gallery, were decorated and furnished by the younger Chippendale in 1800–4, just as Nostell and Harewood had been by his father. Architecturally these rooms are masculine, simple and unaffected. Their furniture is unusual in its design, and reflects the personality of the owner, Sir Richard Colt Hoare, who was a cultivated man, a scholar, traveller and antiquarian.

The library is a long room dominated by a squared carpet based on patterns from a Roman mosaic pavement. The predominant colours are green and old gold. The furniture was delivered from St Martin's Lane in 1804, the very year in which Chippendale's business collapsed. In spite of this there was no falling-off in quality, and each mahogany piece is of excellent workmanship.

94 Thomas Chippendale the younger. Library table. Stourhead, Wiltshire.

This piece has carved philosophers' and sphinx heads, and may have been partly designed by its scholarly owner.

91
92

94

95

95 Thomas Chippendale the younger. Library chair. Stourhead, Wiltshire.

The chair illustrated here is decorated with sphinx heads. The Egyptian head became very common in the later Regency period, but the various pieces of furniture at Stourhead were the first in England to use it.

96 Thomas Chippendale the younger. Two chairs. Stourhead, Wiltshire.

These are two of a set of eight chairs delivered in 1812, when Chippendale was trying to recover his business. They are of a quite original design, and have gilded mouldings.

96